For more laughs get these other LOL books now:

ISBN: 978-1642502329

Squeaky Clean Super Funny Jokes for Kidz

ISBN: 978-1642502367

Squeaky Clean Super Funny School Jokes for Kidz

ISBN: 978-1642502381

Squeaky Clean Super Funny Riddles for Kidz

SQUEAKY CLEAN SUPER FUNNY

KNOCK KNOCK! JOKES

for kidz

LOL!

Written and illustrated by Craig Yoe

mango

CORAL GABLES

Cover Design: Craig Yoe and Clizia Gussoni
Cover Photo/illustration: Craig Yoe
Layout & Design: Elina Diaz

For permission requests, please contact the publisher at:
Mango Publishing Group
2850 S Douglas Road, 2nd Floor
Coral Gables, FL 33134 USA
info@mango.bz

For special orders, quantity sales, course adoptions and corporate
sales, please email the publisher at sales@mango.bz. For trade and
wholesale sales, please contact Ingram Publisher Services at customer.
service@ingramcontent.com or +1.800.509.4887.

Squeaky Clean Super Funny Knock Knock Jokes for Kidz

Library of Congress Cataloging-in-Publication number: 2020933913
ISBN: (print) 978-1-64250-234-3, (ebook) 978-1-64250-235-0
BISAC category code JUVENILE NONFICTION, Humor /
Jokes & Riddles

Printed in the United States of America

DEDICATION

TO GRIFFIN & GRACE

1

SQUEAKY CLEAN

KNOCK KNOCKS

The Name Game

Knock, knock!

Who's there?

Candice.

Candice who?

Candice discussion end and you just open the door?

Knock, knock!

Who's there?

Justin.

Justin who?

Justin from Cleveland, can I sleep over?

Knock, knock!

Who's there?

Della.

Della who?

It's not Della who, it's Delaware!

Knock, knock!

Who's there?

Alfie.

Alfie who?

Alfie really cold—please let me in!

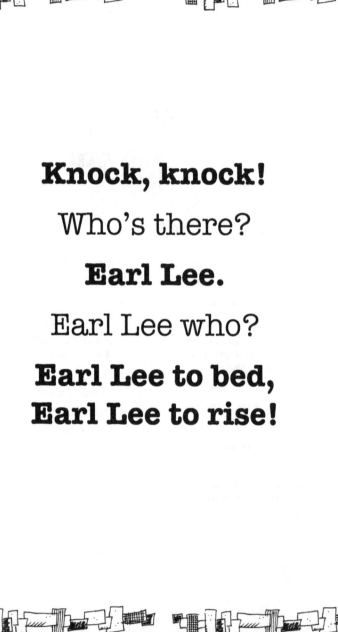

Knock, knock!

Who's there?

Earl Lee.

Earl Lee who?

**Earl Lee to bed,
Earl Lee to rise!**

Knock, knock!

Who's there?

Jim.

Jim who?

Jim mind if I don't answer, that's kind of personal!

Knock, knock!

Who's there?

Oliver.

Oliver who?

Oliver doors are locked, can you let me in?

Knock, knock!

Who's there?

Gabe.

Gabe who?

Gabe my name to the doorman!

Knock, knock!

Who's there?

Al.

Al who?

Al let you know when you open the door!

Knock, knock!

Who's there?

Carrie.

Carrie who?

Carrie me up the stairs, I'm exhausted!

Knock, knock!

Who's there?

Bert.

Bert who?

Bert my dinner, can I eat with you?

Knock, knock!

Who's there?

Allie.

Allie who?

Allie Luyah! You opened the door!

Knock, knock!

Who's there?

Alex.

Alex who?

Alex 'plain if you open the door!

Knock, knock!

Who's there?

Felix.

Felix who?

Felix-cited to meet me?

Knock, knock!

Who's there?

Bertha.

Bertha who?

Happy Bertha to you!

Knock, knock!

Who's there?

Alec.

Alec who?

Alec you, do you like me?

Knock, knock!

Who's there?

Shirley.

Shirley who?

**Shirley you
can guess!**

Knock, knock!

Who's there?

Morry Lee.

Morry Lee who?

Morry Lee, Morry Lee, Morry Lee, Morry Lee, life is but a dream!

Knock, knock!

Who's there?

Hugo.

Hugo who?

Hugo first!

Knock, knock!

Who's there?

Tamara.

Tamara who.

Tamara is only a day away!

Knock, knock!

Who's there?

Les.

Les who?

Les forget the whole thing!

Knock, knock!

Who's there?

Mabel.

Mabel who?

Mabel be here soon!

Knock, knock!

Who's there?

Eliza.

Eliza who?

Eliza wake at night wondering the same thing!

HAR! HAR! HAR!

Knock, knock!

Who's there?

Tim.

Tim who?

Tim you opened the door!

Knock, knock!
Who's there?
Amanda.
Amanda who?
Amanda mow the lawn!

Knock, knock!
Who's there?
Jess.
Jess who?
Jess me!

Knock, knock!
Who's there?
Linda.
Linda who?
**Linda cup of sugar?
I'm baking a pie!**

Knock, knock!
Who's there?
Juno.
Juno who?
**Juno, that's a very
good question!**

Knock, knock!
Who's there?
Betty.
Betty who?
**Betty yet, ask me WHY
I am here!**

Knock, knock!
Who's there?
Alda.
Alda who?
**Alda knocking and
you just NOW answer
the door?!**

Knock, knock!
Who's there?
Anita.
Anita who?
Anita good answer!

Knock, knock!
Who's there?
Stefan.
Stefan who?
Stefan outside so I can give you a big hug!

Knock, knock!
Who's there?
Ellie.
Ellie who?
Ellie-phants never forget!

Knock, knock!
Who's there?
Abby.
Abby who?
Abby makes honey!

Knock, knock!
Who's there?
Pepper.
Pepper who?
Pepper-oni pizza!

Knock, knock!

Who's there?

Ameda.

Ameda who?

Ameda mistake—wrong door!

Knock, knock!
Who's there?
Stan.
Stan who?
Stan back, please, and I'll deliver the pizza!

Knock, knock!
Who's there?
Andy.
Andy who?
Andy jokes just keep on coming!

Knock, knock!
Who's there?
Dora.
Dora who?
Dora bell isn't working so I knocked!

Knock, knock!
Who's there?
Mary Lou.
Mary Lou who?
Mary Lou if you'll say, "I do!"

Knock, knock!

Who's there?

Aladdin.

Aladdin who?

Aladdin the apartment next door sent me!

Knock, knock!

Who's there?

Harley.

Harley who?

**Harley know
you either!**

Who's there?

O'Shea.

O'Shea who?

O'Shea can you see?

Knock, knock!

Who's there?

Allen.

Allen who?

**Allen you a dollar if you
pay me back next week!**

Knock, knock!

Knock, knock!

Who's there?

Harmony.

Harmony who?

**Harmony roads must a
man walk down?**

Knock, knock!

Who's there?

Ringo.

Ringo who?

**Ringo your bell,
no answer, so then
I knocked!**

Knock, knock!

Who's there?

Carmen.

Carmen who?

Carmen let me in!!

Knock, knock!

Knock, knock!

Who's there?

Abel.

Abel who?

Abel to leap tall buildings in a single bound!

Who's there?

Olive.

Olive who?

**Olive you with
all my heart.**

Knock, knock!

Who's there?

Babar.

Babar who?

Babar cut my hair!

Knock, knock!

Who's there?

Howard.

Howard who?

**Howard I'm
supposed to know?!**

Knock, knock!

Who's there?

Otis.

Otis who?

Otis just me!

Knock, knock!

Who's there?

Anna.

Anna who?

Anna one you want!

Knock, knock!

Who's there?

Paul.

Paul who?

**Paul up a seat and let's
have a good talk!**

Knock, knock!

Who's there?

Pat.

Pat who?

Pat my head, I'm your dog come home!

Knock, knock!

Who's there?

Adam.

Adam who?

Adam up and give me my bill!

Knock, knock!

Who's there?

Earl.

Earl who?

Earl be happy to let you know when you open the door!

Knock, knock!

Who's there?

Bea.

Bea who?

Bea my Valentine.

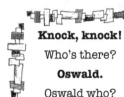

Knock, knock!

Who's there?

Oswald.

Oswald who?

Oswald my key— can you let me in?

29

Knock, knock!

Who's there?

Alfred.

Alfred who?

Alfred I can't answer you now. I'll come back later!

Knock, knock!
Who's there?
Watson.
Watson who?
Watson TV?

Knock, knock!
Who's there?
Hy.
Hy who?
Hy five!

Knock, knock!
Who's there?
Clara.
Clara who?
**Clara the way, I'm
coming in!**

Knock, knock!
Who's there?
Kim.
Kim who?
Kim to me and get a hug!

Knock, knock!

Who's there?

Albee.

Albee who?

**Albee knocking until
you let me in!**

Knock, knock!

Who's there?

Stu.

Stu who?

**Stu many of us
to answer!**

Knock, knock!

Who's there?

Greta.

Greta who?

Greta the cheese!

Knock, knock!

Who's there?

Mort.

Mort who?

**Mort the merrier—
let us in!**

Knock, knock!

Who's there?

Odessa.

Odessa who?

Odessa a good question!

Knock, knock!

Who's there?

Warren.

Warren who?

Warren my gym clothes—wanna go work out?

Knock, knock!

Who's there?

Lena.

Lena who?

Lena out your window and you'll see!

Knock, knock!

Who's there?

Ruth.

Ruth who?

Ruth be known, I haven't a clue!

Knock, knock!

Who's there?

Xavier.

Xavier who?

Xavier questions and open the door!

Knock, knock!

Who's there?

Sid.

Sid who?

Sid down and rest your feet!

Knock, knock!

Who's there?

Olivia.

Olivia who?

Olivia but I'm locked out!

Knock, knock!

Who's there?

Fern.

Fern who?

Fern crying out loud it's good to see you!

Knock, knock!

Who's there?

Onar.

Onar who?

Onar goodness, did I wake you up?

Knock, knock!

Who's there?

Ron.

Ron who?

Ron these parts nobody locks their door!

Knock, knock!

Who's there?

Addie.

Addie who?

Addie body home?

Knock, knock!

Who's there?

Mack.

Mack who?

Mack-aroni and cheese!

Knock, knock!

Who's there?

Francis.

Francis who?

Francis where Paris is!

Knock, knock!

Who's there?

Harry.

Harry who?

Harry up, would you, please—it's raining outside!

Knock, knock!
Who's there?
Hedda.
Hedda who?
Hedda answer but now I forget!

Knock, knock!
Who's there?
Meg.
Meg who?
Meg ya look!

Knock, knock!
Who's there?
Howard.
Howard who?
I'm fine, Howard you?

Knock, knock!
Who's there?
Malcolm.
Malcolm who?
Malcolm you don't recognize me?!

Knock, knock!
Who's there?
Spock.
Spock who?
Spock-ghetti!

Knock, knock!
Who's there?
Ken.
Ken who?
Ken you repeat the question?

Knock, knock!

Who's there?

Mikey.

Mikey who?

Mikey isn't working, can you open the door?

Knock, knock!
Who's there?
Gladys.
Gladys who?
Gladys time for our visit!

Knock, knock!
Who's there?
Brie.
Brie who?
Brie right back!

Knock, knock!
Who's there?
Anna.
Anna who?
Anna-ther knock-knock joke!

Knock, knock!
Who's there?
Ethan.
Ethan who?
Ethan pizza, want a bite?!

Knock, knock!
Who's there?
Sam.
Sam who?
Sam as always!

Knock, knock!

Who's there?

Sandy.

Sandy who?

Sandy beach, let's go swimming!

Knock, knock!

Who's there?

Sabina.

Sabina who?

Sabina ages since we saw each other last!

Knock, knock!

Who's there?

Jethro.

Jethro who?

Jethro the key out the window!

Knock, knock!

Who's there?

Oswald.

Oswald who?

Oswald my tongue!

Knock, knock!

Who's there?

Sheri.

Sheri who?

Sheri your home and I'll share mine!

Knock, knock!

Who's there?

Gino.

Gino who?

Gino that's a good question!

Knock, knock!

Who's there?

Jewel.

Jewel who?

Jewel know when I know!

Knock, knock!

Who's there?

Wilma.

Wilma who?

Wilma knocks be answered soon?

Knock, knock!

Who's there?

Ken.

Ken who?

Ken I get back to you on that later?

Knock, knock!

Who's there?

Hadja.

Hadja who?

Hadja head if you recognize me!

Knock, knock!

Who's there?

Keanu.

Keanu who?

Keanu just let me in, I'm tired of knocking!

Knock, knock!

Who's there?

Lee.

Lee who?

Lee me look on my driver's license and find out!

Knock, knock!

Who's there?

Les.

Les who?

Les is more!

Knock, knock!

Who's there?

Sofia.

Sofia who?

Sofia me, please, I haven't eaten all day!

Knock, knock!

Who's there?

Sherwood.

Sherwood who?

Sherwood like to know, I can understand that!

Knock, knock!

Who's there?

Saul.

Saul who?

Saul's well that ends well!

HAR! HAR! HAR!

Knock, knock!

Who's there?

Luke.

Luke who?

Luke out your window and you'll see!

Knock, knock!

Who's there?

Bert.

Bert who?

Bert laid an egg on my head!

Knock, knock!

Who's there?

Abraham.

Abraham who?

Abraham and mayo sandwich, please!

Knock, knock!

Who's there?

Scott.

Scott who?

Scott to be my little grandson. My how you have grown!

Knock, knock!

Who's there?

Ada.

Ada who?

Ada ham and mayo, thanks!

Knock, knock!

Who's there?

Keith.

Keith who?

Keith me goodbye, and I'll try not to cry!

Knock, knock!

Who's there?

Daryl.

Daryl who?

Daryl be plenty of time for your questions when you open the door!

Knock, knock!

Who's there?

Sheila.

Shiela who?

Sheila be right here; she's coming up the walk!

Knock, knock!

Who's there?

Theodore.

Theodore who?

Theodore on the bus goes open and shut!

Knock, knock!

Who's there?

Wade.

Wade who?

Wade—it's on the tip of my tongue!

Knock, knock!

Who's there?

Allison.

Allison who?

Allison to your questions, if you listen to my answers!

Knock, knock!

Who's there?

Rina.

Rina who?

Rina this bell and nobody answered, so I knocked!

WHO'S THERE?!

Knock, knock!

Who's there?

Ben.

Ben who?

Ben there, done that!

Knock, knock!

Who's there?

Dawn.

Dawn who?

Dawn ask me any questions and I'll tell you no lies!

Knock, knock!

Who's there?

Ozzie.

Ozzie who?

Ozzie ya later, alligator!

Knock, knock!

Who's there?

Vaughn.

Vaughn who?

**Vaughn two,
buckle my shoe!**

Knock, knock!

Who's there?

Elle.

Elle who?

Elle-O-L.

Knock, knock!

Who's there?

Vera.

Vera who?

**Vera all the
flowers gone?**

Knock, knock!

Who's there?

Hal.

Hal who?

Hal about letting me in?

Knock, knock!

Who's there?

Dewey.

Dewey who?

Dewey have to have this discussion every time?!

Knock, knock!

Who's there?

Atlas.

Atlas who?

Atlas it's time we meet again!

Knock, knock!

Who's there?

Vanna.

Vanna who?

Vanna hear another knock knock joke?

Knock, knock!

Who's there?

Gwen.

Gwen who?

Gwen will you open the door?

Knock, knock!

Who's there?

Harriet.

Harriet who?

Harriet to the door please!

Knock, knock!

Who's there?

Ivan.

Ivan who?

Ivan to the door with your pizza!

Knock, knock!

Who's there?

Vanessa.

Vanessa who?

Vanessa time you see me I hope you'll remember!

Knock, knock!
Who's there?
Fred.
Fred who?
Fred I've forgotten my name again!

Knock, knock!
Who's there?
Theodore.
Theodore who?
Theodore or the window—I'm coming in when you open up!

Knock, knock!
Who's there?
Phyllis.
Phyllis who?
Phyllis in on how you've been doing!

Knock, knock!
Who's there?
Seymour.
Seymour who?
Seymour when you let me in!

Knock, knock!
Who's there?
Grace.
Grace who?
Grace you to the end of the street!

Knock, knock!
Who's there?
Sharon.
Sharon who?
Sharon is carin'!

Knock, knock!
Who's there?
Max.
Max who?
Max me laugh these knock knock jokes!

Knock, knock!
Who's there?
Ida.
Ida who?
Ida name but I forgot what it is!

Knock, knock!
Who's there?
Noah.
Noah who?
Noah good knock knock joke? I got nothing!

Knock, knock!
Who's there?
Annie.
Annie who?
Annie body home?

Knock, knock!

Who's there?

Harry.

Harry who?

Harry up I'm holding all these groceries!

Knock, knock!

Who's there?

Plato.

Plato who?

Plato ice cream and cake, please!

Knock, knock!

Who's there?

Lorne.

Lorne who?

Lorne time no see!

Knock, knock!

Who's there?

Otto.

Otto who?

Otto know by now, I'm your own brother!

Knock, knock!

Who's there?

Leif.

Leif who?

Leif the door unlocked next time!

Knock, knock!

Who's there?

Emma.

Emma who?

Emma momma with you?

Knock, knock!

Who's there?

Violet.

Violet who?

Violet my friend borrow my key, can you let me in?

Knock, knock!

Who's there?

Greta.

Greta who?

Greta lakes are good for swimming!

Knock, knock!

Who's there?

Frank.

Frank who?

Frank you very much!

Knock, knock!

Who's there?

Aida.

Aida who?

Aida piece of pizza!

Knock, knock!

Who's there?

Elvis.

Elvis who?

Elvis-ulize you opening the door!

Knock, knock!

Who's there?

Beth.

Beth who?

Beth you can't guess!

Knock, knock!

Who's there?

Theodore.

Theodore who?

Theodore is now open!

Knock, knock!

Who's there?

Ima.

Ima who?

Ima Popeye the sailor man!

Knock, knock!

Who's there?

Kent.

Kent who?

Kent really say, does anyone really know their own self?

Knock, Knock!
Zoo's There?
Animal Knocks

Knock, knock!

Who's there?

Gorilla.

Gorilla who?

**Gorilla my dreams
come true!**

Knock, knock!

Who's there?

Bears.

Bears who?

**Bears the
party happening?!**

Knock, knock!

Who's there?

Lion.

Lion who?

**Lion the rug so I can
wipe my feet!**

Knock, knock!

Who's there?

Goose.

Goose who?

**Goose see who's
at the door!**

Knock, knock!

Who's there?

Owl.

Owl who?

Owl let ya know when you open the door!

Knock, knock!

Who's there?

Rabbit.

Rabbit who?

Rabbit up I'll take it!

Knock, knock!

Who's there?

Gopher.

Gopher who?

Gopher a bike ride with me?

Knock, knock!

Who's there?

Goat.

Goat who?

Goat to the door and let me in!

Knock, knock!

Who's there?

Goose.

Goose who?

I give up, who?!?

Knock, knock!

Who's there?

Owls say.

Owls say who?

Yes, they do!

Don't Knock
Your Veggies

Knock, knock!
Who's there?
Carrot.
Carrot who?
Carrot to let me in?

Knock, knock!
Who's there?
Kale.
Kale who?
Kale to let me in?

Knock, knock!
Who's there?
Bean.
Bean who?
Bean a long time no see!

Knock, knock!
Who's there?
Lettuce.
Lettuce who?
Lettuce get acquainted.

Knock, knock!

Who's there?

Asparagus.

Asparagus who?

Asparagus the questions, don't you know you own family?!

Knock, knock!

Who's there?

Okra.

Okra who?

Okra-homa is the Sooner State!

Knock, knock!

Who's there?

Radish.

Radish who?

Radish or not, here I come!

Knock, knock!

Who's there?

Turnip.

Turnip who?

Turnip the music; I can't hear it in my apartment!

Knock, knock!

Who's there?

Leeks.

Leeks who?

Leeks in your roof? I'm the repairman!

Knock, knock!

Who's there?

Gourd.

Gourd who?

Gourd dog barked at me, but I got through!

Knock, knock!

Who's there?

Peas.

Peas who?

Peas to meet you!

Knock, knock!

Who's there?

Beetroot.

Beetroot who?

Beetroot-full, you really don't recognize me!?

Knock, knock!

Who's there?

Maize.

Maize who?

Maize the force be with you!

Knock, knock!

Who's there?

Shallots.

Shallots who?

Shallots to catch up on!

Knock, knock!

Who's there?

Chives.

Chives who?

Chives been running errands and I forgot my house key!

Knock, knock!

Who's there?

Cantaloupe.

Cantaloupe who?

Cantaloupe, so I wanted to give you my wedding invitation.

Knock, knock!
Who's there?
Dill.
Dill who?
I'm the real Dill.

Knock, knock!
Who's there?
Snap pea.
Snap pea who?
Snap pea dresser!

Knock, knock!
Who's there?
Bean.
Bean who?
Bean on vacation.

The Rest of the Menu

Knock, knock!

Who's there?

Pasta.

Pasta who?

Pasta my bedtime, open the door!

Knock, knock!

Who's there?

Walnut.

Walnut who?

Walnut here, so I knocked on the door!

Knock, knock!

Who's there?

Bacon.

Bacon who?

Bacon a cake— want a piece?

Knock, knock!

Who's there?

Doughnut.

Doughnut who?

Doughnut open the door and I can't come in!

Knock, knock!

Who's there?

Wafer.

Wafer who?

Wafer a while but I'm home now!

Knock, knock!

Who's there?

Water.

Water who?

Water you doing, can you come out and play?

Knock, knock!

Who's there?

Gouda.

Gouda who?

Gouda question!

Knock, knock!

Who's there?

Grape.

Grape who?

Grape question!

Knock, knock!

Who's there?

Orange.

Orange who?

Orange ya gonna open the door?

Knock, knock!

Who's there?

Icing.

Icing who?

Icing a song if you open the door!

Knock, knock!

Who's there?

Orange juice.

Orange juice who?

Orange juice gonna open the door?

Knock, knock!

Who's there?

Cheese.

Cheese who?

Cheese don't feed the animals!

Knock, knock!

Who's there?

Soup.

Soup who?

Supergirl!

Knock, knock!

Who's there?

Apple.

Apple who?

Apple the door, but it won't open!

Knock, knock!

Who's there?

Pizza.

Pizza who?

Pizza your mind!

Knock, knock!

Who's there?

Honeydew.

Honeydew who?

Honeydew you have toast for me when I come home?

5

Oh, the Places
You'll Knock!

USA

Knock, knock!

Who's there?

Utah.

Utah who?

Utah me at school and told me to come over!

Knock, knock!

Who's there?

Bronx.

Bronx who?

Yes, I've got the tickets—let's go see the animals!

Knock, knock!

Who's there?

Missouri.

Missouri who?

Missouri loves company.

Knock, knock!

Who's there?

Maine.

Maine who?

Maine you look!

Knock, knock!
Who's there?
Alaska.
Alaska who?
Alaska my mama!

Knock, knock!
Who's there?
Yukon.
Yukon who?
Yukon ask but I'll never tell!

Knock, knock!
Who's there?
Oregon.
Oregon who?
Oregon, but I'm here!

Knock, knock!
Who's there?
Ohio.
Ohio who?
Ohio feeling!

Knock, knock!
Who's there?
Hawaii.
Hawaii who?
Hawaii, I'm doing good myself!

Around the World

Knock, knock!

Who's there?

Europe.

Europe who?

Europe and at 'em?

Knock, knock!

Who's there?

Kenya.

Kenya who?

Kenya please let me in?

Knock, knock!

Who's there?

Rwanda.

Rwanda who?

Rwanda know? Open the door!

Knock, knock!

Who's there?

Samoa.

Samoa who?

Samoa questions like that I'd be happy to answer!

Knock, knock!

Who's there?

Spain.

Spain who?

Spain to me what you're asking, and I'll try my best to answer!

Knock, knock!

Who's there?

Sweden.

Sweden who?

Sweden the pot, and I'll tell you my name!

Knock, knock!

Who's there?

Togo.

Togo who?

Togo or not to go—that is the question!

Knock, knock!

Who's there?

Uganda.

Uganda who?

Uganda be asking me that! I'm your own mother!

Knock, knock!

Who's there?

Tonga.

Tonga who?

Tonga tied, let me try and answer!

Knock, knock!

Who's there?

Syria.

Syria who?

Syria later, alligator!

Knock, knock!

Who's there?

Turkey.

Turkey who?

Turkey is not where it should be; unlock the door please!

Knock, knock!

Who's there?

Sweden.

Sweden who?

Sweden sour chicken is my favorite food!

Knock, knock!

Who's there?

Ukraine.

Ukraine who?

Ukraine your neck out the window and you'll see who I am!

Good Sport Jokes!

Soccer! You'll Get a Kick Out of This One...

Knock, knock!

Who's there?

Goalie.

Goalie who?

Goalie against the tree to rest during half-time!

Going Bats for Baseball!

Knock, knock!

Who's there?

Pitcher.

Pitcher who?

Pitcher this: a no-hits game!

Basketball Belly Laughs!

Knock, knock!

Who's there?

Dunk.

Dunk who?

Dunk ask me how I did it, but I just scored!

Golf Tee-Hee!

Knock, knock!

Who's there?

Fore.

Fore who?

Fore score and seven games ago!

A Tennis Tease

Knock, knock!

Who's there?

Tennis.

Tennis who?

Tennis the number after nine!

Hockey Schmockey!

Knock, knock!

Who's there?

Goalie.

Goalie who?

I'm goalie oriented!

A Running Joke!

Knock, knock!

Who's there?

Sprint.

Sprint who?

Sprint is due today— gotta run to the bank, then to the landlord's!

A Couple Jokes to Bowl You Over

Knock, knock!

Who's there?

Strike.

Strike who?

Strike up the band!

Knock, knock!

Who's there?

Spare.

Spare who?

Spare me the corny jokes!

7

Knocks around
the Clock

Knock, knock!

Who's there?

Boo.

Boo who?

Please don't cry; I didn't mean to upset you!

Knock, knock!

Who's there?

Icon.

Icon who?

Icon stop laughing!

Knock, knock!

Who's there?

Barber.

Barber who?

Barber black sheep, have you any wool...

Knock, knock!

Who's there?

Blue.

Blue who?

Aw, why are you crying?

Knock, knock!

Who's there?

Canoe.

Canoe who?

Canoe PLEASE open the door?

Knock, knock!
Who's there?
Sofa.
Sofa who?
Sofa so good!

Knock, knock!
Who's there?
Zany.
Zany who?
Zany body home?

Knock, knock!
Who's there?
Cash.
Cash who?
I prefer walnuts.

Knock, knock!
Who's there?
iPad.
iPad who?
iPad a hard day. Let me in so I can sleep!

Knock, knock!
Who's there?
House.
House who?
House the weather today?

Knock, knock!
Who's there?
Dish.
Dish who?
Dish is ridiculous!

Knock, knock!

Who's there?

Waiter.

Waiter who?

Waiter second, it'll come to me!

Knock, knock!

Who's there?

Teacher.

Teacher who?

Teacher kids to open the door!

Knock, knock!

Who's there?

Wish.

Wish who?

Wish you wouldn't ask me all these questions!

Knock, knock!

Who's there?

Juicy.

Juicy who?

Juicy on your calendar I'm supposed to come over tonight?

Knock, knock!

Who's there?

Ivory.

Ivory who?

Ivory sorry to bother you!

Knock, knock!

Who's there?

Butcher.

Butcher who?

Butcher key under the doormat next time!

Knock, knock!

Who's there?

Dancer.

Dancer who?

Dancer my friend is blowing in the wind!

Knock, knock!

Who's there?

Ears.

Ears who?

Ears me, there's you. Open the door, thank you!

Knock, knock!

Who's there?

Mister.

Mister who?

Mister when she came to my house, so now I'm coming here!

Knock, knock!

Who's there?

Pajamas.

Pajamas who?

Pajamas around me— I need a hug!

Knock, knock!

Who's there?

Ear.

Ear who?

Ear I am, sorry I'm late!

Knock, knock!

Who's there?

Wish.

Wish who?

Wish you wouldn't ask me all these questions!

Knock, knock!

Who's there?

User.

User who?

User ask a lot of questions!

Knock, knock!

Who's there?

Pasture.

Pasture who?

Pasture bedtime. Sorry I woke you!

Knock, knock!

Who's there?

Grammar.

Grammar who?

Grammar is married to Grampa!

Knock, knock!

Who's there?

Dishes.

Dishes who?

Dishes is the last time I'm gonna knock!

Knock, knock!

Who's there?

Game.

Game who?

Game over to see you!

Knock, knock!

Who's there?

Fangs.

Fangs who?

Fangs for opening the door!

Knock, knock!

Who's there?

Broken.

Broken who?

Broken doorbell so I knocked!

Knock, knock!

Who's there?

Star.

Star who?

Star your engines, we're off to the races!

Knock, knock!

Who's there?

Saturn.

Saturn who?

Saturn your porch waiting for you for an hour!

Knock, knock!

Who's there?

Lurking.

Lurking who?

Lurking for my keys and can't find them!

Knock, knock!

Who's there?

Oink.

Oink who?

Hey, are you a pig or an owl?!

Knock, knock!

Who's there?

Thumb.

Thumb who?

Thumb body please open the door!

Knock, knock!

Who's there?

Fauna.

Fauna who?

Fauna isn't working so I came over!

Knock, knock!

Who's there?

Kook.

Kook who?

Kook who clock!

Knock, knock!

Who's there?

Noise.

Noise who?

Noise to meet you!

Knock, knock!

Who's there?

Major.

Major who?

Major look!

Knock, knock!
Who's there?
Jupiter.
Jupiter who?
Jupiter key under the mat?

Knock, knock!
Who's there?
Data.
Data who?
Data good question!

Knock, knock!
Who's there?
Fleas.
Fleas who?
Fleas open the door!

Knock, knock!
Who's there?
Keypad.
Keypad who?
Keypad out as long as I could—can I come in now?

Knock, knock!
Who's there?
Needle.
Needle who?
Needle some money for the bus ticket!

Knock, knock!
Who's there?
Police.
Police who?
Police stop with the questions already!

Knock, knock!

Who's there?

Handsome.

Handsome who?

Handsome sandwiches out the window, I'm hungry!

Knock, knock!
Who's there?
Ya.
Ya who?
Ya who and yippie ki yay!

Knock, knock!
Who's there?
Snow.
Snow who?
Snowbody—it was just the wind!

Knock, knock!
Who's there?
Who.
Who who?
Best owl imitation EVER!

Knock, knock!
Who's there?
Spell.
Spell who?
W-H-O.

Knock, knock!
Who's there?
Know.
Know who?
Of course, I know— you're the one with the questions!

Knock, knock!
Who's there?
Say.
Say who?
Who!

Knock, knock!

Who's there?

Wheelbarrow.

Wheelbarrow who?

Wheelbarrow your car and bring it right back!

Knock, knock!

Who's there?

Knives.

Knives who?

Knives to meet you!

Knock, knock!

Who's there?

Snow.

Snow who?

Snow good answer to that question!

Knock, knock!

Who's there?

Who! Now will you please open the door?

Knock, knock!

Who's there?

Phew.

Phew who?

Phew, that was a close one!

Knock, knock!

Who's there?

Ask.

Ask who?

Ask her while, crocodile!

Knock, knock!

Who's there?

Ceiling.

Ceiling who?

Ceiling Girl Scout cookies! Want some?

Superheroes and Villains Knock, Knock, Pow! Wham!

Let's Start with Superman's Favorites

Knock, knock!

Who's there?

Kent.

Kent who?

Kent let anybody know my secret identity!

Knock, knock!

Who's there?

Pa Kent.

Pa Kent who?

Pa Kent my car in front of your house. Hope I don't get a ticket!

Knock, knock!

Who's there?

Lois.

Lois who?

Lois the opposite of high!

Knock, knock!

Who's there?

Jimmy.

Jimmy who?

Jimmy the lock, I can't get in the door!

Knock, knock!

Who's there?

Lex Luthor.

Lex Luthor who?

Lex, Lu-thor attitude!

Knock, knock!

Who's there?

Locket.

Locket who?

Locket in the sky!

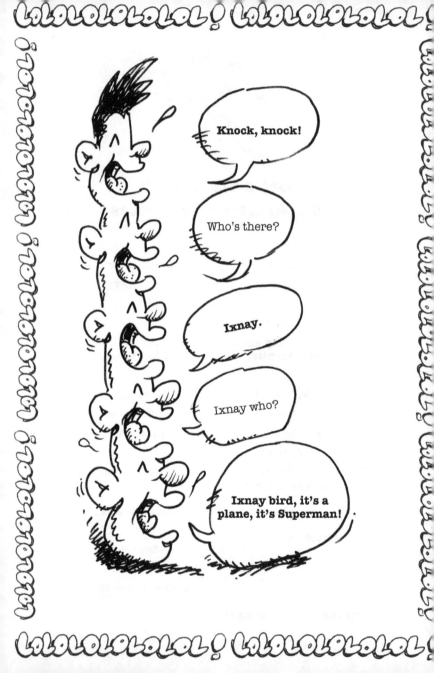

Now for the Caped Crusader's Faves

Knock, knock!

Who's there?

Batman.

Batman who?

Batman is almost as good as tennis—so grab a racket and birdie and let's play!

Knock, knock!

Who's there?

Robin.

Robin who?

Robin the rich to give to the poor!

Knock, knock!

Who's there?

I'm Alfred.

I'm Alfred who?

I'm Alfred the Joker's back to his evil deeds!

Thor Likes These...

Knock, knock!
Who's there?
Odin.
Odin who?
Odin you some money!

Knock, knock!
Who's there?
Thor.
Thor who?
Thor was open so I came right in!

More Marvelous Marvel Heroes

Knock, knock!
Who's there?
Spidey.
Spidey who?
Spidey light on so I stopped to visit!

Knock, knock!
Who's there?
X-Men.
X-Men who?
X-Men the pan, do you want them scrambled?

Knock, knock!

Who's there?

Loki.

Loki who?

Loki in your window, and I saw that you were home!

Knock, knock!

Who's there?

Wasp.

Wasp who?

Wasp up, dude?!

Knock, knock!

Who's there?

Iron Man.

Iron Man who?

Iron Man to your house, man, to get here quick, man!

Knock, knock!

Who's there?

Dr. Strange.

Dr. Strange who?

Dr. Strange his back so he can't see you today!

And Finally, a Bedtime Knock Knock Joke

Good night.

About the Author

Vice magazine has called Yoe the "Indiana Jones of comics historians." *Publisher Weekly* says he's the "archivist of the ridiculous and the sublime" and calls his work "brilliant." *The Onion* calls him a "celebrated designer," *The Library Journal* says, "a comics guru." BoingBoing hails him "a fine cartoonist and a comic book historian of the first water." Yoe was creative director/vice president/general manager of Jim Henson's Muppets, and a creative director at Nickelodeon and Disney. Craig has won multiple Eisner Awards and the Gold Medal from the Society of Illustrators. Yoe has the record for writing and illustrating more kids' joke books than anyone on the planet.

mango

Mango Publishing, established in 2014, publishes an eclectic list of books by diverse authors—both new and established voices—on topics ranging from business, personal growth, women's empowerment, LGBTQ studies, health, and spirituality to history, popular culture, time management, decluttering, lifestyle, mental wellness, aging, and sustainable living. We were recently named 2019's #1 fastest growing independent publisher by *Publishers Weekly*. Our success is driven by our main goal, which is to publish high quality books that will entertain readers as well as make a positive difference in their lives.

Our readers are our most important resource; we value your input, suggestions, and ideas. We'd love to hear from you—after all, we are publishing books for you!

Please stay in touch with us and follow us at:

Facebook: Mango Publishing
Twitter: @MangoPublishing
Instagram: @MangoPublishing
LinkedIn: Mango Publishing
Pinterest: Mango Publishing

Sign up for our newsletter at www. mangopublishinggroup.com and receive a free book!

Join us on Mango's journey to reinvent publishing, one book at a time.

CPSIA information can be obtained
at www.ICGtesting.com
Printed in the USA
BVHW030347011020
590032BV00004B/4